T0198744

PILGRIMAGE POEMS

Poetry to encourage reflection and growth

RANDY STOLTZ

WestBow Press books may be ordered through booksellers or by contacting:

WestBow Press
A Division of Thomas Nelson & Zondervan
1663 Liberty Drive
Bloomington, IN 47403
www.westbowpress.com
1 (866) 928-1240

Scripture quotations are from Revised Standard Version of the Bible, copyright © 1946, 1952, and 1971 National Council of the Churches of Christ in the United States of America. Used by permission. All rights reserved worldwide.

ISBN: 978-1-9736-8108-3 (sc)
ISBN: 978-1-9736-8109-0 (e)

Print information available on the last page.

Library of Congress Control Number: 2019920039

WestBow Press rev. date: 12/26/2019

WESTBOW
PRESS®
A DIVISION OF THOMAS NELSON
& ZONDERVAN

As long as I've known Randy he has been on a spiritual journey. As a creative musician, songwriter and poet, he has given authentic voice to the groanings and wonderings of his soul; to know God and himself and to live life as an image bearer of Christ in ways that encourage others to see themselves as God sees them – beloved, cherished and called. As Randy's Spiritual Director I have come to understand what it means to companion someone on such a journey. I am humbled and thankful to walk with him. Thanks Randy.

- Sarah Page

I have been witness to Randy's personal evolution for some time now, and his work in this collection is a clear reflection of the open-minded and deep spiritual connection that he is seeking passionately.

- John Ackley, Counselor

TABLE OF CONTENTS

ACKNOWLEDGEMENTS

No one lives in a vacuum. I am indebted to too many people to possibly mention here. I will mention a few. First, to my mom, who imparted a sense of family, love and home. She took me to church when I was very young and when tucking me in bed at night taught me I could pray to God. It won't be long now, Mom. I love you. To my amazing wife, Nadine, who has suffered the brunt of my imperfections and shortcomings. Thank you for your patience and understanding… I love you! To Doug Alfred, my friend of 30 years, my older "brother" in the faith. Thank you for all your support in too many ways to enumerate here. To my sister, Connie, who has provided a growing close bond of both family and faith in Christ, I love you. To my brother, Mark, we have grown much closer caring for Mom. I love you. To Sarah Page my spiritual director, worship pastor & friend. Thank you for making this journey much better!

To all my friends at the Kroc Center, thank you for your zest and commitment to live life fully, especially Lydia McGranahan and Jim Weins. Who else could devise such torturous workouts and make it fun?! To Emily Spicer, co-worker, computer wizard and friend. I couldn't have done this without you! To all my work associates at Highway Trailer Sales: Roger, Teri and Matt, Ron, Clyde, Kevin, Dan, Doyle, Tim C, Tim T., Chris, Mark, Karmen, and McKynna. You can not work with folks and they not see your weaknesses and shortcomings. Thank you for your patience and love!

Finally to the many gifted writers : Thomas Merton, Richard Rohr, Martin Laird, Cynthia Bourgeault, Kathleen Singh, Ken Wilber, Maggie Ross, Chris and Phileena Heuertz to mention a few. I have been profoundly impacted by their books and feel presumptuously by extension to be a friend …thank you for going before me and writing about the journey. Little of the content of these poems are original with me. I have borrowed phrases and thoughts from them and put them in some meager, lyrical form as I journaled poetically, in efforts to birth through writing what was transpiring in my heart.

INTRODUCTION

This book of poems, which I wrote last year, is both the culmination of many years of processing in my life and also a launching pad of sorts, a new beginning. I was raised in a Methodist church. Our family moved to a different town my senior year of high school. This move was a catalyst towards personal faith in Christ. I went to a bible college to serve God and demonstrate my appreciation and sincerity for all He had done for me.

Working in a church as a job was never a good fit for me. It never felt right, so I didn't. Although I was quite heavily involved in church life and programs through the years, I felt like I was on the outside looking in. This was true both personally with God and socially with others. Little then did I realize that this was mainly due to a cultural mindset and God's purposes. I've since learned that a integral component of Western thinking, culture and education is based upon dualistic thought, specifically whereby one imagines themselves to be an outside observer studying external objects to draw conclusions about the world they live in.

Through the years several scriptures intuitively resonated with me whenever I read them. "For you are great and doing wondrous things, you are God alone. Teach me your ways, Oh, Lord that I may walk in your truth; unite my heart to fear your name…. (Psalm 86:10-12)." My heart was divided. Like, a dog chasing its own tail, thinking it was an external, separate object to be chased and caught, I was trying to draw closer to God and catch Him. I just never could get close enough for long. Scripture said I was united with Christ, even seated in heavenly places with Him, (Romans 6:5, Ephesians 2:5-6), but that was not my consistent experience. I was no more separated from God than a dog is from his tail he tries to catch! Somehow I knew this deep down, but my rational mind wouldn't allow me to enjoy this reality. Any scriptures that talked about God rescuing us from a bad predicament, be it a miry bog or our difficult enemies and setting us in a broad open place struck a strong, resonate chord within me. I longed to get out of my small, myopic, fearful self. I knew I should, but how to do this escaped my decades-long, diligent efforts (Psalms 18:16-19, Psalms 40:2).

By far though, the capstone scripture verses that I returned to for 30 plus years, are found In Genesis 2:8-9, 15-17 and 3:1-13. When I first was captured by these verses I was in wonder of the fathomless depths I intuitively perceived there. I couldn't put my finger on it exactly, but a spiritual reality/realm's gateway was there. Like a scuba diver sighting several beautiful fish in very clear water, so clear that their actual depth is much farther down than it appears, these verses have drawn my attention. Yet, I had not experienced them very much until these last two very difficult years. I started reading about Christian contemplatives, mystics and other meditative disciplines. I was amazed at what I was reading! Where had this been all my life? My training, my struggles, my studies, my life all began to assemble together like a thousand piece jigsaw puzzle in the completion stage.

I discovered from my readings that it was not but a few years ago through the advances in quantum physics, mathematics and other new developing sciences that the many dualisms imbedded in western thought for the past twenty five centuries were being eliminated. Quantum physics had discovered it was impossible to verify reality by measuring it! It was not accurate to believe in the classic, scientific approach we were taught in school that we were outside and separate from what we saw and observed. Rather it had been proven that we were in fact an integral part of what we observed . There was in fact a bigger more complete picture (1 Corinthians 2:9). As I grew in my ability to quiet my mind I was delighted to find a much bigger realm to live and move and have my being! (Acts 17:28) Those passages in Genesis came to life. I transitioned from just the tree of the knowledge good and evil to the more encompassing tree of life (Rev. 22:2). We cease from our labors and enter into His rest (Hebrews 4:1-3). Science confirmed what the mystics long ago knew. We are not outside of God. We are in him. Please enjoy these poems. They have been a joy to express as I my heart slowly journeys from an awareness of separation from God to union with God in Christ (Philippians 2:12).

Blessings,

Randy

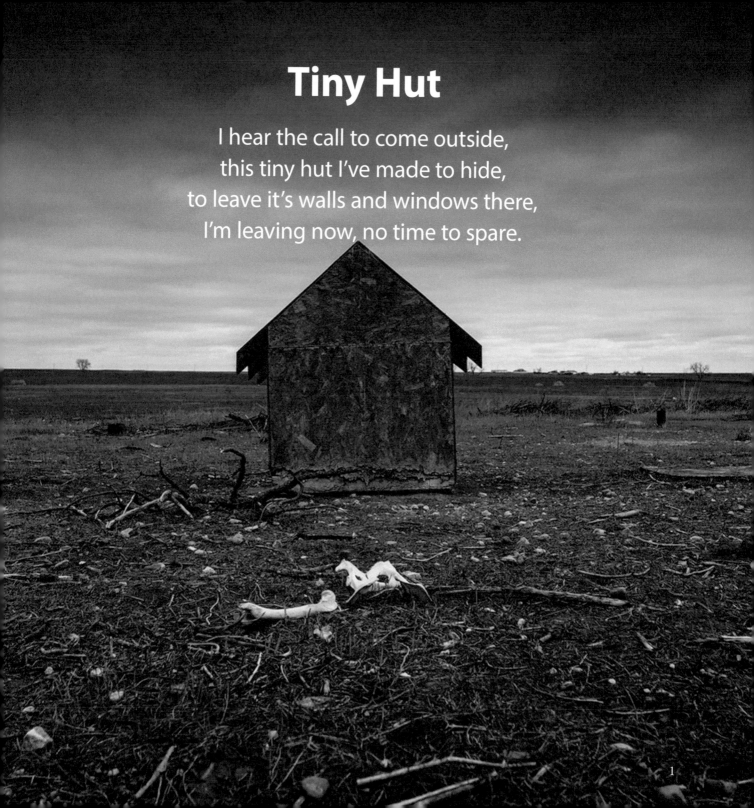

Tiny Hut

I hear the call to come outside,
this tiny hut I've made to hide,
to leave it's walls and windows there,
I'm leaving now, no time to spare.

A Walk

I went on a walk,
to bring outside inside,
by mountains and trees,
there treasure troves hide.
The rivers flow free,
there is nothing to buy...
I went on a walk to bring outside inside.

Come for a Walk

Where am I going? I admit I'm not sure,
but that kind of knowing is not what I yearn.
I hear His voice calling to me,
here I am walking towards what I can't see.

Where I grew up, I left long ago behind,
where I am going, I have yet to find,
but whom I have found for sufficiency,
said, "come for a walk, come follow me."

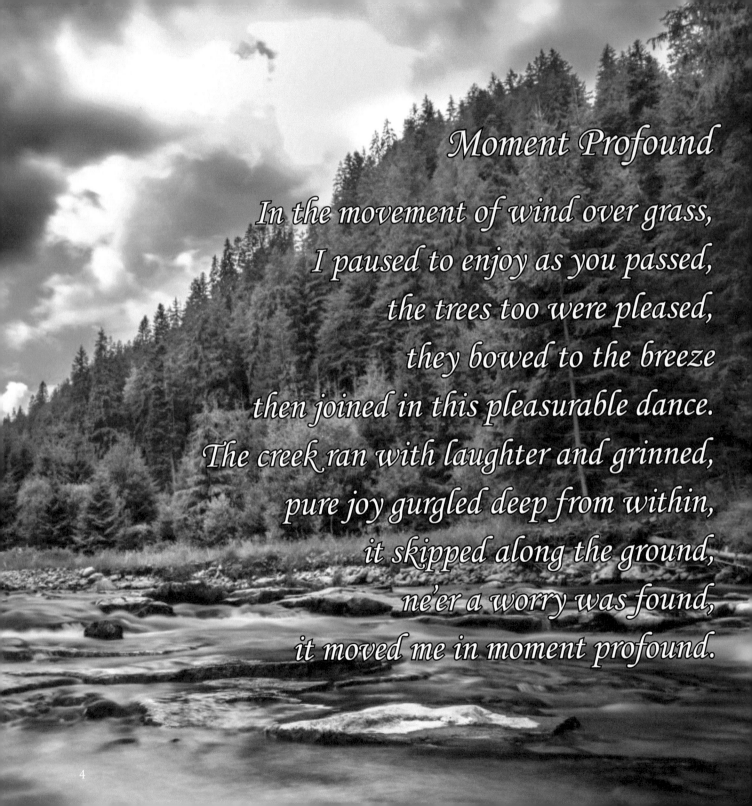

Moment Profound

In the movement of wind over grass,
I paused to enjoy as you passed,
the trees too were pleased,
they bowed to the breeze
then joined in this pleasurable dance.
The creek ran with laughter and grinned,
pure joy gurgled deep from within,
it skipped along the ground,
ne'er a worry was found,
it moved me in moment profound.

Waiting for eternity

Waiting for eternity, I missed it just go by,

as life is more than physical, so also I can die,

to life occurring yesterday or waiting it to come,

I'm finding out eternity is already now begun.

Breathe

I breathe Him in and
let breath out,
He swirls amongst my soul,
the dance of life,
grins with delight,
and bids me to let go.
I find I've come, t'where
life's begun,
and lives with every breath.
My heart's sustained,
as I remain, to do what dancers
do the best.

God's Breath

If the breath I breathe,
created me, can my breath
be but divine?
The rhythm of each "in" and "out",
attests I'm His and He is mine.
His heart's desire is we be one,
this desire He has made so.
May each breath I breathe,
a reminder be,
of what His breath has done.

Objects Apart?

I know there are objects,
some far and some near,
and from our perspective,
we are separate it appears,
but microscopes and science,
when they measured the small,
discovered that matter,
is not like that at all.

Why I am anxious and
why I have fear,
a lot of my efforts are
attempts to get near.
But, just as a branch can
be but part of the tree,
this I'm discovering is
true also of me.

Still Waits the Spider

Still waits the spider, alert undisturbed,
though sounds come a calling, most are unheard.
Dinner is coming to say alive,
will be some small thing, hope for a fly.
Silk-spun trap webbing there to imbed,
thoughts as they're coming, fast from our heads.
Interior silence waiting them come,
spring into action, soon will be done.
See one come flying, eager to pounce,
wrap in silk silence, fear nary an ounce.
Stillness surrounding, buzzing is done,
awareness was waiting supper to come.

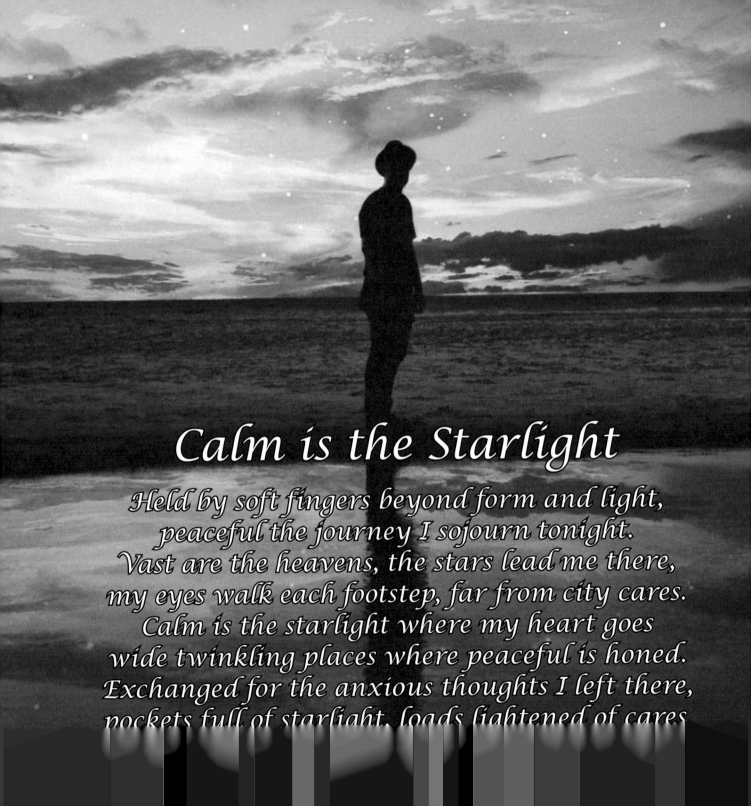

Calm is the Starlight

Held by soft fingers beyond form and light,
peaceful the journey I sojourn tonight.
Vast are the heavens, the stars lead me there,
my eyes walk each footstep, far from city cares.
Calm is the starlight where my heart goes
wide twinkling places where peaceful is honed.
Exchanged for the anxious thoughts I left there,
pockets full of starlight, loads lightened of cares

Long Walks

I love long walks, not
just for what I can see,
but for all that I can't.
The seen whispers
of the unseen.
What lies behind the
crows' calls, the birds'
songs, the tall
firs' reach, the skies'
and clouds' and
sun's dance. They
each in turn talk
softly of that. And I
mesmerized, take it all
in 'til wonder again
lays hold of me. I
walk 'til I've nearly
forgotten whether I'm
young or I'm old,
then I turn and
wander back.

journey home

A walk to a peaceful place is where I go,
there streams flow surrendered for all
that they know, is how to embark on their
trip to the sea, home to the
greater is their destiny.
Traveling while singing, their songs inspire,
for all that they know, is
alone what they aspire.
Their journeys' guide them
to where they need be,
the more I observe them,
this more clearly I see.

Befriended by Silence

Silence introduced himself
to me lately,
a stranger of whom I knew little.
Somehow he gradually
convinced me
that we had very
much in common.
I was doubtful and
afraid at first but very
tired of feeling alone.
Surprisingly soon we
became close friends.
He said I was just ready.
Funny how you can
live so close to someone
a long time and know so little about them.
Now we meet often. I look forward to our times
a lot and can't imagine life without his friendship.

If I Could Grasp God

If I could grasp God, what would He be like?
Would He be dark, would He be light?
Would He be tall, would He be short?
If I could grasp God, what would I report?
What does one say of one who is unseen?
What does one imagine, how does one dream?
To grasp God is an order to tall,
descriptions fall short of knowing at all.
What I do know is based on my need,
how I am made is how I proceed.
My need for love moves me to see,
If I could grasp God, He'd be loving of me.

Inner Eyes

Good morning God, I view you now,
with eyes before not seen. I learned somehow
that seeing, is more than it might seem.
It's not only trees and mountains, that greet
our outer eyes, but how they tell of your secret that,
behind their forms you lie.

15

Snakes and God

The sun doesn't care whether you've been good or bad,
it still rises and sets each day.
Capernicus scratches his head and rolls his eyes.
The planets don't revolve around the earth,
nor we around our worries.
Snakes and God wonder when we too
will shed our smalls skins,
and enjoy being larger.

Living Like Madmen

We wander like madmen,
because we don't see,
anxious and worried,
oh, where can He be?
All along He's been buried,
a deep treasure inside,
where peaceful is plenty,
there waiting to find.

We run into living,
just like a brick wall,
stumble off course,
towards many a fall,
repentantly sorry,
worried again,
He's always there waiting,
when we come to
dead ends.

One day we wake up,
with new opened eyes,
all outward seeking,
exchanged for surprise.
He comes out of hiding,
when He does please,
along on our journey,
waving 'til we see.

God was Gone

I thought God was gone, searched everywhere,
searched each crevice of mind, but alas He was not there.
Bleak was my outlook, cold was my heart,
I never was taught, finding God was such an art.
I could not find Him, about me was noise,
worse than most kids, enamored with their toys.
My head full of buzzing, like a hive large with bees,
forsaken I was certain, God had decided to leave.
Sullen and morbid, depressed and in despair,
how could I find, this God who wasn't there
Where should I search for the place God would hide,
especially since He was so much larger than I?
Exhausted from searching, strength had no choice but to go,
no interest in diversions and all they could show.
The laughter of gallows, rang loud in the air,
echoed off mountains, God wasn't there.
Then in my silence, I heard a small "peep",
louder it grew, the more I grew weak.
Eager to practice what I had just learned,
God had never left me, so He could not return.
All of my searching, had been on the outside,
meanwhile back home, inside He lay reclined.
Eating so little, I had become thin,
then I discovered God's dwelling was within.

18

A Fish Out of Water

Like a fish who lives in water,
or an otter in the sea,
is there more today in living,
than just worrying, out there for me?
Is there something I'm missing,
Is there a place someone might tell?
I hunger for a homeland,
where worrying does not dwell.

The Onset of Winter

Watching my thoughts,
like the falling of leaves,
at the onset of winter,
from the cold
temperatures' freeze.
When the trees become dormant,
stark brown and quite bare,
at the onset of winter,
all that's left is God there.

The Roses Have Faded

The roses have faded,
don't worry you and I,
although often struggle,
will bloom and not die.
So please don't you worry,
nor let your heart fear,
as sure as tomorrow,
I love you my dear.

The morning is coming,
'tis something we know,
we will grow older, more
wrinkles will show.
Yet, we'll watch together,
this one truth is clear,
as sure as tomorrow, I
love you my Dear.

Ladder to Heaven

All around now are windows,

all I'd found were brick walls,

the ladder before me, rose high

and most tall. Stretching towards heaven,

the climb now had come,

ascent up to home, each step of a rung.

Awakened from dreaming,

or had it been real?

Beyond all our thinking,

or five senses can reveal,

discernment for traveling,

from the false to the real,

manna from heaven,

food for my meals.

Love Emanating

Love hummed with motion, then
sprung forth (as) with wings,
traveled fast as sound waves,
their purpose to bring,
form into fruition, plans into profound,
creation gave birth to skies,
water and hard ground.

Light into darkness, which
made it most bright,
whispers to shouting,
proclaiming with might,
love's emanation, 'til
all did appear,
forms' celebration, the
unseen is quite near.

Hope is for holding,
what sight cannot see,
faith is for viewing all the
unseen. Love emanating
through shapes to
make clear, God's
very presence,
closer than near.

The Unity of Opposites

The unity of opposites came
knocking at my door,
one side was delightful, the
other most abhorred.

The more I fought the negative,
it's better side I missed,
until I saw the gist of both,
and gave them each a kiss.

What Have We Lost?

What makes us think, we could leave them behind,
all that they learned, we being blind?
What have we lost that they already found,
all that they could tell us, if we kept around?
Doesn't it hurt, when we don't learn from their pain?
When we trust in ourselves, what is it we gain?
Oh, but to listen, the older we grow,
to those who have gone first, before we could go.
To hear the wise tales of those who've gone before,
I am eager to hear them, please tell me some more.

Country Flowers

In the country grow some flowers,
a long a side of road,
their faces upwards to heaven,
a scene no one else might know.
They shine without a struggle,
to be just who they are,
no need to be the tallest tree,
or envy the brightest star.

Swaying with the breezes,
they move to His delight,
what else could they be doing,
exerting all their intent and might?
How else could they be pleasing,
formed flowers made to be?
Consider country flowers,
a long side a road,
swaying in the breeze.

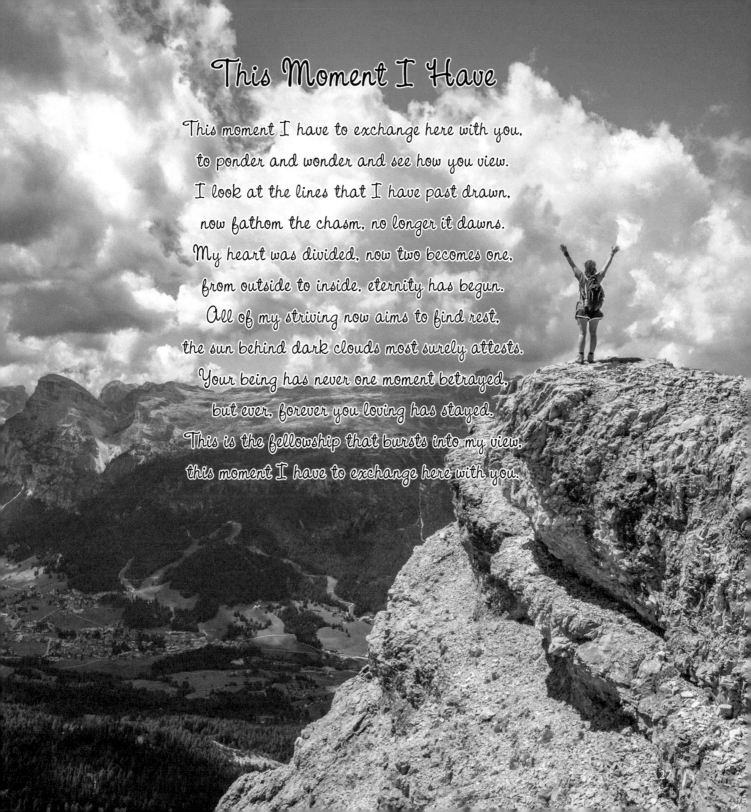

This Moment I Have

This moment I have to exchange here with you,

to ponder and wonder and see how you view.

I look at the lines that I have past drawn,

now fathom the chasm, no longer it dawns.

My heart was divided, now two becomes one,

from outside to inside, eternity has begun.

All of my striving now aims to find rest,

the sun behind dark clouds most surely attests.

Your being has never one moment betrayed,

but ever, forever you loving has stayed.

This is the fellowship that bursts into my view,

this moment I have to exchange here with you.

Poultice of Nature

I love to go hiking far in the woods,
far from the "oughts", away
from the "shoulds".
I love to go trekking to simply just "be",
away from my worries, swept
clean by the breeze.
I love to go gazing nights at the stars,
escape from home's ceilings,
that's where they are.
Floating in heaven, suspended in air,
brightest in darkness,
surpassing all cares.

Grand are the heavens,
bright are the stars,
vast are the forests,
such solace they are.
A poultice of
nature, held right
'round my soul,
sound soothing silence
on trails where I go.

Why we are Silent

Comfort for depression, worry or doubt,
why we are silent waiting it out, why we are
watching, eager to see, life ever flowing,
greater than these. Why we are silent, eager
to hear, life ever present, closer than near.

God in Nature's Clothing

How was it I missed for so long,
that birds flying, clouds scampering, winds
frolicking and the sun emanating, was God
disguised in nature's clothing,
showing himself to me?

The many shades of weather tell me plainly
that his stedfast love is new
in endless ways every
morning. When I grow weary
of dreary cold days,
does not then the sun's sudden
appearance cheer
me more than if it had been sunny all a long?
For these endlessly changing sceneries
of weather I am thankful!

Paints on a Palette

Each one of us is an artist, assigned a work supreme,
not with paint on canvas, or form of clay, or rock as means.
Our substance is our living, moving, breathing being,
yielded to our Master, in awe what we might be.
We are not our own perfection, but trust in someone else,
assigned a life for living, not merely for ourselves...
Like paints placed on a palette, His
soul and ours mixed fine,
we then become his painted artworks,
of God and human combined.

Behind This Veil

Oh thinking mind that loves to grasp,
with grip that hates to
fail, Oh could it be,
that all perceived, is just
in front the veil,
which wraps around our mortal minds,
preventing what we see.
Yet content of our
inmost heart, behind this veil there be,
the presence of our living God,
residing there to see.

Penguins Don't Fly

Penguins don't fly, theirs are short wings,
struggle with flapping, flight not their thing.
Where can they fly, where can they go?
Water their jet stream, wet skies far below.
Flight with my Father, beyond rational thoughts,
seldom such matters rarely are taught.
Hearts are for heaven, flight for the soul.
If one would be flying, that's where one must go.

Ordinary Days

There's rareness in the ordinary,
but we seek to get away,
not seeing what we're given,
we crave another day,
one we esteem that's better, for the
adventures that we long...
we miss the treasures in today, to
which the ordinary belongs.

We are on safari, not for
trophies which to kill,
but game in unknown tangles
requiring much different skills.
We are all out hunting for the
mysterious tucked away,
that lies there hid in secret
in our ordinary days.

Tombstone

I sat beside a tombstone, to wonder
what it meant,
for certain was my outcome when my
time had been all spent.
Since this was conclusive as all
around was plain to see,
it best to die before I die was the
thought that came to me.

The sooner that I ended, was the
sooner I'd be gone,
to leave my faults not cling to false, of
these concepts I've grown fond.
I've grown to be excited about death's
possibilities, to cross to the other side,
where after death I'm going to be.

But if I died before I did, what would it be
like now? Was this the death
for wheat to die, to fall into the ground? As
I looked all about me there were
tombstones all around. This then I
decided, I would die before they laid me
down. I looked more at those tombstones,
the more I looked it seemed not
bad, to die to all I'd created for a better life
at hand. So I died beside that
tombstone on that ordinary day, it was the
best decision, I've since made
often along my way.

Lightning Speed

With what lightning speed,
our minds can race,
all around time and space,
yet defies their range of skill,
is to rest and be quite still.

The Thought of Time

I sit down to work it through,
the thought of time,
how I view,
how the present
remains unseen,
choked by
past hurts and
schemes.
How the
future crowds
now out,
shrouds of fear,
angst and doubts.
Cloaks press near
to cover now,

extinguish joy, replace
with scowls.
Just the same as placed
outside,
from the rest
where I abide.
I sit down
to work it
through,
the thought
of time, how I
view.

Simple Joy

The perching of a bird,
to bring it's gift to God,
greets me in the morn,
with it's song at dawn.
What is it in it's heart,
that moves it so to sing,
which bathes me
in it's mirth,
from joy so simply
drawn?

Wide is the Sky

No words need be spoken, wide is the sky,
objects forsaken, open and high.
Gentle clouds drifting, absent of fear,
peaceful breeze blowing, lovely to hear.
Hearts long for silence,
high sail cloud crafts,
Landscapes are calling
beckoning back.

Tall trees teach daily to touch the sky,
broader horizons delighting the eyes.
Smaller is growing, expansive the sea,
narrowness going, departure, flees.
Oceans spread in the distance,
boundaries fall down, nature
surrounding 360° around.

Surrender

Side to side's the motion,
back and forth all sing,
synergy's vibration,
surrender of our being.
Come listen to this music,
that yielding always brings.
Living from our true center,
comes down to this one thing.

Posted Sentries

All around were posted sentries,
habitual thoughts formed to survive,
yet long had passed those dangers,
still they kept me locked inside.
So I approached them with sound reason,
but my freedom they denied.
I pouted for a season 'til one day I realized,
I need not heed their orders,
nor their antiquated lies.

I neared them afraid and anxious,
that beyond them I couldn't go,
thus far in all my living,
their presence was all I'd ever known.
They told me as I drew closer, a storm lie
certain just a head, but when I saw out beyond them,
there were only blue skies over head.
I passed them in amazement, not one laid a hand on me,
much more than I imagined, were there wonders to be seen.
I turned and waved good-bye then, to those thoughts that
had shut me in, and thanked them for their service,
for their time had come to it's end.

41

Shiny Metal

I saw some shiny metal, it
glittered much like gold,
I flew down and gathered it
with maneuvers swift and bold.
I lined my nest with several
pieces, then reveled
with much delight,
to see it's reflective beauty,
gleaming brightly in the light.

The sun set for the
evening, the gleaming
was all gone,
preparing for the
nighttime I perceived
than perhaps
something wrong.
Discomfort was not
a little, sleep ran all
night 'til it was lost,
when came the dawn of
morning, all that metal
I'd long since tossed!

What learned I from this nighttime, of
collecting metal shiny bright?
What seems much worth the having (can)
end in long and sleepless nights.
Consider more than the surface of bright and shiny things,
the objects of our desiring can lead
to sleeplessness and pain.

darling, you are a work of art

Hurricane of Words

Be hind ou r veils He's wai ting, all
our   chat ter, all   our s w ir l,
all our en dless minds pa rading,
all our hur rica nes o f wor ds.
Onc e those whir l winds ha ve sub sided,
can we lea ve our har ried minds,
to fi nd a pla ce of re spite, lea ve
our fre nzied mi nds b e hi nd?

Come meet a different knowing,
than in school we were ever heard,
not taught in math or science or all
other subjects that we learned.
Come listen to the silence,
come glean all it can teach.
Behind our veils He's waiting,
right now within our reach.

The Meadow

The meadow still, called me until, I eagerly could go, beyond the rush, into it's rush, that nature only knows. The wind and breeze, my soul appeased, they rocked me to and fro. I heard a brook and paused to look, it murmured over me. The sun-baked grass, like pretty lass, asked me to stay, not go. What could say I, nor care to try, but watch the wild flowers as they grow? This healing place where time's erased, and deeper depths are shown. To spirit yield, in sovereign field, while sunset bathes in softest glow. Oh, meadow fair, who has called me there, you've saved my tempest soul. Forever woo and please pursue, caress me with your care. Oh, place serene, almost a dream, you transport my weary soul. Call me again, my dearest friend, for I will surely go.

44

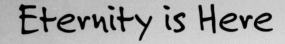

Eternity is Here

Tomorrow is the same as today,
as thoughts of the moment
linger and stay, on more of the
sights and more of the sounds,
eternity is here when more
present is found.
Stopping the race letting things
go, stepping aside, watching
the flow, of all of the thoughts,
I once confused to be me,
infinite mercy helps me to see.
Infinite sights, infinite sounds, all
of them say heaven abounds,
not in the future or sweet bye
and bye, eternity is here,
when more present is found.
The fullness of time can come into view,
when how what is seen, is slowly renewed,
with acres of beauty unending abound....,
eternity is here, when more
present is found.

Wind Currents

Wind Currents rising, gliding through air,
brushing past branches, revealing they're there.

Sounding so soft, like
the utterance of sighs,
bringing a freshness,
soon realized.

Lifting up gliding, birds on the wing,
who float on the power, the invisible brings.
Riding on whispers, held high above,
transported by breezes of of upholding love.

Who can live fully without the current of winds,
blowing and cleansing cobwebs within?
Inhaling, exhaling swirls'round a tired-weary soul.
Who could survive? No one I know.

Simple Presence

"A presence too simple to be absent",
too simple to be cast off and ignored,
a presence too simple to be missing,
an image intact when we're first born.
No question that all sin and are sinners,
but what is the target most often missed?
That sin was our prime disposition,
not fitting our Father's kiss.

True, all we have sinned and are sinners,
but who were we before the fall?
Our road astray led to our pardon,
those forgiven most receive
(grace) most of all.
That which we could never work for,
that which we all greatly need.
Sons and daughters of His labor,
formed and filled with His identity.

This Place

This place I am going to before I was born,
before this ol' body felt tattered and worn.
This place I am going to is calling to me,
nearer than in childhood, Its come closer I see.
Nearer than far away, friend more than foe,
gentler than suffering, with grace it's adorned.
Most of my longings are eager to be,
in this place I am going to before I was born.
Party of parties, reunions sublime,
all of my friends, we're together and fine.
All of our yesterdays, like wool they've been shorn,
in this place I am going to, before I was born.

Printed in the United States
By Bookmasters